75 Yummy Okra Recipes

(75 Yummy Okra Recipes - Volume 1)

Sharon Brown

Content

75 Awesome Okra Recipes

***

---

1. 'Momma Made Em' Chicken And Sausage Gumbo

Serving: 10 | Prep: 20mins | Ready in:

Ingredients

- 1 (3 pound) whole chicken
- 1/2 cup all-purpose flour
- 1/2 cup vegetable oil
- 1 (10 ounce) package frozen chopped onions
- 1 (10 ounce) package frozen green bell peppers
- 5 stalks celery, finely chopped
- 1 tablespoon Cajun seasoning (such as Tony Chachere's), or to taste
- 2 whole bay leaves
- 1 (28 ounce) can diced tomatoes
- 1 pound fully-cooked smoked beef sausage (such as Hillshire Farm®), sliced
- 1 (10 ounce) package frozen sliced okra
- salt and black pepper to taste

Direction

- In a big pot, partially put lightly salted water. Place the chicken in it. Bring it to a boil. Reduce the heat to a simmer. For about 1 hour, cook until the juices run clear and the chicken meat is no longer pink. Remove the chicken from the broth. Allow the chicken to cool by crack opening the carcass. Set the chicken broth aside. When it is already cool, separate the meat from the bones. Set it aside.
- Make a roux while waiting for the chicken to simmer. In a large heavy saucepan, whisk the vegetable oil and the flour over medium-low heat. Stir and cook the mixture for 20 to 30 minutes until the roux turns into a rich chocolate brown color. Watch it constantly to avoid burning.
- Once the roux turns to desired color mix the bay leaves, Cajun seasoning, bell peppers, celery and the onions. For about 45 minutes, simmer until the vegetables are tender. Stir occasionally in between. Add the beef sausage, diced tomatoes and the reserved chicken broth. For about 1 hour, simmer until the mixture has thickened. Stir occasionally in between.
- Add the okra and the reserved chicken meat. For 30 to 40 minutes, cook and simmer until the flavor has blended and the okra is tender. Stir occasionally in between.

Nutrition Information

- Calories: 437 calories;
- Total Fat: 32.2
- Sodium: 835
- Total Carbohydrate: 14.5
- Cholesterol: 67
- Protein: 21.4

---

2. Afghan Okra

Serving: 4 | Prep: 10mins | Ready in:

Ingredients

- 2 tablespoons vegetable oil
- 1 onion, thinly sliced
- 2 tablespoons tomato paste
- 1 pound okra, sliced in 1/4 inch pieces
- 1 teaspoon ground turmeric
- salt and black pepper to taste
- 2 cups water

Direction

- Heat vegetable oil in skillet on medium low heat. Mix onions in; cook for about 15 minutes till dark brown and soft. Mix tomato paste in till there are no lumps. Add okra; sprinkle pepper, salt and turmeric. Put water in; boil on high heat. Lower heat to medium low. Simmer for 15-20 minutes till sauce is slightly thick and okra is very tender. Season with pepper and salt to taste again; serve.

Nutrition Information

- Calories: 127 calories;
- Total Fat: 7.1
- Sodium: 79
- Total Carbohydrate: 15.2
- Cholesterol: 0
- Protein: 3.3

3. Aunt Lillian's Pickled Okra

Serving: 72 | Prep: 40mins | Ready in:

Ingredients

- 1 quart white vinegar
- 1 1/3 cups water
- 1/3 cup salt
- 3 pounds small okra, stems trimmed
- 6 whole chile peppers
- 6 cloves garlic, peeled
- 1 tablespoon mustard seed
- 6 (1 pint) sterilized canning jars with lids and rings

Direction

- In a saucepan, heat the salt, water and vinegar over medium-high heat. Bring it to a boil. Once done, remove from heat.
- For at least 5 minutes, sterilize the lids and the jars in boiling water. In each of the hot, sterilized jars, pack one garlic clove, 1 pepper and the okra tightly. Over the top, sprinkle

mustard seeds. In each jar, pour the vinegar mixture. At the top, leave 1/2 inch space. To remove any food residue, wipe the rims of the jars with a moist paper towel. Put the lid. Screw in rings.
- At the bottom of a big stockpot, place a rack. Fill it water, just halfway through. Bring it to a boil. Use a holder to lower the jars into the boiling water. Between the jars, leave a 2-inch space. If necessary, to bring the water to at least a 1 above the top of the jars pour more boiling water in. Bring it to a rolling boil. Cover the pot. Process for 10 minutes.
- Transfer the jars to a cloth-covered or wood surface from the stockpot. Leave several inches space between the jars to let it cool. Press the top of each lid with your finger once cool to make sure that the seal is tight. Make sure the lid does not move up or down when pressed. Leave it in a dark and cool area for at least 4 weeks before opening.

Nutrition Information

- Calories: 9 calories;
- Total Carbohydrate: 1.8
- Cholesterol: 0
- Protein: 0.5
- Total Fat: 0.1
- Sodium: 2

4. Baked Chicken And Okra

Serving: 10 | Prep: 10mins | Ready in:

Ingredients

- 2 cups uncooked white rice
- 1 (3 pound) whole chicken, cut into pieces
- 2 (28 ounce) cans whole peeled tomatoes, chopped, juice reserved
- 2 cups small fresh okra
- 2 bay leaves
- 5 cups chicken broth

- salt and black pepper to taste

Direction

- Preheat the oven at 175°C or at 350°F.
- At the bottom of a 10x15 inches baking dish, spread the rice. On top of the rice, layer the bay leaves, okra, tomatoes and the chicken pieces. Over the ingredients, pour the reserved tomato juice and the broth. Season it with pepper and salt.
- Cover it. Bake until the chicken is tender and falling off its bone, for two hours. Once done, remove the bay leaves. Put it in large bowls with plenty of sauce and rice. Serve.

Nutrition Information

- Calories: 348 calories;
- Total Fat: 10.8
- Sodium: 283
- Total Carbohydrate: 39
- Cholesterol: 58
- Protein: 23

5. Bamia

Serving: 6 | Prep: 15mins | Ready in:

Ingredients

- 2 tablespoons olive oil
- 1 pound beef steak, cut into cubes
- 1 onion, chopped
- 2 cloves garlic, crushed
- 8 cups water
- 1 (14.5 ounce) can crushed tomatoes
- 1 pound frozen okra
- 4 ounces tomato puree
- 1 teaspoon coriander
- 1/2 teaspoon ground cumin
- 1/8 teaspoon allspice
- 1 dash lemon juice
- salt and ground black pepper to taste

Direction

- In big pot, heat oil on medium high heat; mix and cook beef cubes in hot oil for about 10 minutes till all sides are browned. Add garlic and onion to beef; mix and cook for 3-5 minutes till slightly tender and fragrant.
- Mix pepper, salt, lemon juice, allspice, cumin, coriander, tomato puree, okra, tomatoes and water into beef mixture; boil. Lower heat to low. Simmer for about 2 hours till sauce thickens.

Nutrition Information

- Calories: 214 calories;
- Protein: 15.7
- Total Fat: 11.4
- Sodium: 206
- Total Carbohydrate: 14.1
- Cholesterol: 40

6. Bamieh (Middle Eastern Okra Stew)

Serving: 8 | Prep: 20mins | Ready in:

Ingredients

- 2 tablespoons vegetable oil
- 2 large onions, chopped
- salt and ground black pepper to taste
- 2 pounds cubed lamb stew meat
- 3 tablespoons ground cinnamon
- 1 1/2 teaspoons ground cumin
- 1 1/2 teaspoons ground coriander
- 1 1/2 tablespoons garlic paste
- 5 (14.5 ounce) cans canned diced tomatoes, drained
- 1 1/2 tablespoons tomato paste
- 2 beef bouillon cubes
- 4 cups boiling water
- 2 pounds frozen sliced okra

Direction

- Heat vegetable oil in big pot on medium heat. Mix black pepper, salt and onion in. Mix and cook for about 10 minutes till onion is light golden brown and soft.
- Add garlic paste, coriander, cumin, cinnamon and lamb. Cook for 10-15 minutes on medium heat till lamb begins to brown, occasionally mixing. Mix tomato paste and tomatoes in; mix and cook for 5 more minutes.
- In 4 cups boiling water, melt beef bouillon cubes. Put broth into pot with lamb. Mix okra in. Cover okra with water if needed; cover. Simmer, occasionally mixing, for 30 minutes. Uncover. Cook till stew hits preferred thickness and lamb is very tender for another 45 minutes – 1 hour.

Nutrition Information

- Calories: 262 calories;
- Total Carbohydrate: 22.6
- Cholesterol: 53
- Protein: 21.6
- Total Fat: 8.3
- Sodium: 779

---

7. Beef And Okra Bamia

Serving: 6 | Prep: 20mins | Ready in:

Ingredients

- 2/3 cup olive oil
- 1 tablespoon salt
- 1 pound beef top sirloin, cut into 1-inch cubes
- 1/2 large onion, chopped
- 6 cloves garlic, minced
- 2 (10 ounce) cans tomato sauce
- 1 tablespoon tomato paste
- 1 (10 ounce) package frozen okra, thawed
- 2 cups water
- 1 1/2 tablespoons ground coriander

- 1 teaspoon ground white pepper
- 2 teaspoons ground cumin
- salt to taste
- 1 jalapeno pepper, thinly sliced

Direction

- In a big pot, heat olive oil on high heat. Sprinkle 1 tbsp. salt on steak cubes; mix and cook meat in hot oil with garlic and salt for about 5 minutes till meat is seared. Lower heat to medium; mix and cook for about 3 more minutes till meat is browned. Take steak pieces out; put aside.
- Mix tomato paste and tomato sauce into same pot. Stir cumin, white pepper, coriander, water and okra in; boil. Season with extra salt. Lower heat to low. Simmer for 30-45 minutes till okra is tender. Put beef pieces into bambia; simmer for about 10 minutes till flavors merge. Garnish with jalapeno pepper slices.

Nutrition Information

- Calories: 366 calories;
- Protein: 16
- Total Fat: 29.1
- Sodium: 1707
- Total Carbohydrate: 12.4
- Cholesterol: 33

---

8. Bhindi Masala (Spicy Okra Curry)

Serving: 4 | Prep: 20mins | Ready in:

Ingredients

- 4 cups okra, cut into 1-inch pieces
- 1 tablespoon olive oil
- 1 teaspoon cumin seeds
- 1 onion, chopped
- 2 tomatoes, diced
- 1 teaspoon curry powder

- 1 teaspoon salt

Direction

- In a big, microwave-safe dish, put the okra n. For 6 minutes, cook it in the microwave over high heat.
- In a big skillet, heat the cumin seeds and the olive oil together over medium heat. Cook until the cumin seeds turn golden brown and swells. For 3 minutes, fry the onions in the heated oil. Put the tomatoes in and allow another 3 minutes to cook. Mix the okra and season it with salt and the curry powder. For about 3 more minutes, stir and cook the mixture until hot then serve.

Nutrition Information

- Calories: 100 calories;
- Total Fat: 3.9
- Sodium: 597
- Total Carbohydrate: 15.8
- Cholesterol: 0
- Protein: 3.4

9. Bhindi Subzi (Okra Stir Fry)

Serving: 4 | Prep: 20mins | Ready in:

Ingredients

- 2 tablespoons mustard oil
- 1 pound okra, cut into 1/4-inch pieces
- 5 cloves garlic, minced, or more to taste
- 1 teaspoon cumin seeds
- 1 large red onion, thinly sliced
- 1 1/2 teaspoons diced ginger
- 1 teaspoon ground turmeric
- 1 teaspoon garam masala
- 2 tomatoes, diced
- 1/2 teaspoon amchoor (dried mango powder)
- salt to taste
- 2 tablespoons chopped cilantro, or to taste

Direction

- In big nonstick skillet, heat mustard oil on medium heat. Add cumin seeds, garlic and okra; mix and cook for 5-10 minutes till okra isn't sticky. Add ginger and onions; cook for 3-5 minutes till onions slightly soften. Mix turmeric powder in; cook for 30 seconds. Mix garam masala in; cook for about 30 seconds.
- Mix amchoor powder and tomatoes into skillet; cook for about 1 minute till tomatoes begin to soften. Take skillet off heat; cover. Let rest for about 10 minutes till flavors merge. Season with salt; garnish with cilantro.

Nutrition Information

- Calories: 133 calories;
- Sodium: 56
- Total Carbohydrate: 15.8
- Cholesterol: 0
- Protein: 3.5
- Total Fat: 7.6

10. Briam (Greek Mixed Vegetables In Tomato Sauce)

Serving: 12 | Prep: 30mins | Ready in:

Ingredients

- 4 tomatoes
- 1/2 cup olive oil
- 2 tablespoons red wine vinegar
- 2 tablespoons white sugar
- 1/3 cup chopped fresh parsley
- 1/3 cup chopped fresh mint
- 1/3 cup chopped fresh basil
- 2 tablespoons fresh oregano
- 1/4 cup capers
- 2 cloves garlic
- salt and ground black pepper to taste
- 2 tablespoons olive oil
- 2 onions, sliced

- 2 potatoes, sliced
- 2 eggplant, sliced
- 3 zucchini, sliced
- 3 green bell peppers, sliced
- 2 cups okra

Direction

- Set the oven at 350°F (175°C) and start preheating. In a food processor's bowl, put garlic, capers, oregano, basil, mint, parsley, sugar, red wine vinegar, 1/2 cup of olive oil and three of the tomatoes; process to form a fresh tomato sauce. Season with black pepper and salt; set aside. Chop the remaining tomatoes and set aside.
- Place a skillet on medium heat and heat 2 tablespoons of olive oil, cook onions while stirring for around 10 minutes till slightly golden.
- Combine together the fresh tomato sauce, the reserved chopped tomato, okra, bell peppers, zucchini, eggplant, potatoes and onions; arrange the mixture on a large baking pan. Mix in a little water if necessary so the sauce just covers the vegetables.
- Bake for around 1 hour in the preheated oven or till all the vegetables turn tender.

Nutrition Information

- Calories: 177 calories;
- Total Fat: 11.6
- Sodium: 97
- Total Carbohydrate: 17.7
- Cholesterol: 0
- Protein: 2.7

11. Caribbean Fish Soup

Serving: 8 | Prep: 35mins | Ready in:

Ingredients

- 2 whole fish, scaled and cleaned, or more to taste
- 1 lemon, juiced
- 8 cups water
- 4 green bananas, chopped
- 1 pound pumpkin, cut into 1-inch pieces, or more to taste
- 2 potatoes, chopped
- 2 ears corn, cut into 1-inch pieces
- 4 ounces carrots, cut into 1/2-inch pieces
- 1/2 cup chopped okra
- 4 scallions, chopped
- 1 hot chile pepper
- 2 cloves garlic, chopped
- 1 teaspoon salt
- 1 teaspoon ground black pepper
- 4 sprigs fresh thyme, leaves stripped

Direction

- Use lemon juice to rinse fish; drain.
- Boil water in big bowl and add fish; simmer for about 30 minutes till soft then strain fish. Keep broth. Cool fish. Remove bones and try to keep big fish pieces intact.
- Boil broth; add thyme, pepper, salt, garlic, chile pepper, scallions, okra, carrots, corn, potatoes, pumpkin and green bananas. Boil again. Lower heat to low. Simmer for about 10 minutes till potatoes are nearly tender. Mix fish in; simmer for about 5 more minutes till flavors merge.
- Take soup off heat. Before serving, let stand for about 30 minutes then throw chile pepper.

Nutrition Information

- Calories: 203 calories;
- Total Fat: 3.3
- Sodium: 338
- Total Carbohydrate: 35
- Cholesterol: 26
- Protein: 11.6

12. Chef Kiran's Okra Stir Fry

Serving: 4 | Prep: 15mins | Ready in:

Ingredients

- 2 tablespoons vegetable oil
- 1 pound small okra
- 1/2 teaspoon ground turmeric
- 1 clove garlic, chopped
- 1/2 teaspoon chopped fresh ginger
- 2 onions, cut into quarters
- 2 roma (plum) tomatoes, cut into quarters
- 1 tablespoon chopped fresh cilantro

Direction

- Heat a big skillet or wok with vegetable oil on medium-high heat then put in the okra and stir-fry for 3 minutes or until soft and golden brown in color. Put the stir-fried okra on a plate.
- Put turmeric into the hot oil and heat for 1-2 minutes or until it is fragrant. Mix in the ginger, tomatoes, onions and garlic then stir-fry for approximately 10 minutes or until the onions are soft. Add in the stir-fried okra into the onion mixture. Top off with cilantro.

Nutrition Information

- Calories: 125 calories;
- Sodium: 13
- Total Carbohydrate: 14.8
- Cholesterol: 0
- Protein: 3.2
- Total Fat: 7.1

13. Chicken Gumbo Over Rice

Serving: 6 | Prep: 35mins | Ready in:

Ingredients

- 1/4 cup olive oil, divided
- 1/2 pound Italian sausage, cut into 1/4-inch slices
- 1/4 cup all-purpose flour
- 1 pound skinless, boneless chicken breasts, cut into 1/2-inch strips
- 1 cup chopped onion
- 1 cup diced green bell pepper
- 1 cup chopped celery
- 2 tablespoons minced jalapeno peppers
- 1 teaspoon ground paprika
- 1 1/2 cups 1/4-inch fresh okra slices
- 1 cup chicken broth
- 1/2 cup white wine
- 2 cups cooked white rice

Direction

- Heat 2 tbsp. oil in big skillet on medium heat and add sausage. Mix and cook for about 10 minutes till browned. Put on paper towel-lined plate with a slotted spoon.
- In skillet, heat leftover 2 tbsp. oil. Add flour; cook, constantly whisking, for 8-10 minutes till dark brown. Add paprika, jalapeno peppers, celery, green bell pepper, onion and chicken; mix and cook for 7-8 minutes till onion is soft.
- In a slow cooker, pour chicken mixture, then mix white wine, chicken broth, okra, and cooked sausage,.
- Cover. Cook for 7-8 hours on low till flavors merge. Serve on rice.

Nutrition Information

- Calories: 373 calories;
- Cholesterol: 55
- Protein: 22.5
- Total Fat: 18.1
- Sodium: 526
- Total Carbohydrate: 25.2

14. Chunky Vegetarian Vegetable Soup (Fast And Easy)

Serving: 10 | Prep: 15mins | Ready in:

Ingredients

- 2 tablespoons olive oil
- 1/2 onion, chopped
- 3 stalks celery, chopped
- 2 cloves garlic, minced
- 4 cups vegetable broth
- 1 (15 ounce) can tomato sauce
- 4 carrots, peeled and cut into 1/4-inch rounds
- 2 baking potatoes, cut into bite-size pieces
- 1 cup frozen corn
- 1 cup frozen shelled edamame (green soybeans)
- 1 cup frozen sliced okra
- 2 leaves kale, roughly chopped
- salt to taste
- 1 teaspoon ground black pepper

Direction

- In big pot, heat olive oil on medium heat. Mix and cook celery and onion in hot oil for about 5 minutes till onion is translucent and soft.
- Mix garlic into onion mixture; mix and cook for 2-3 more minutes till fragrant.
- Put tomato sauce and vegetable broth into pot then simmer for about 10 minutes.
- Mix potatoes and carrots through broth; simmer for 10-15 more minutes till carrots are tender.
- Drop kale, okra, edamame and corn into soup; simmer for 5-10 more minutes till okra is tender. Season with pepper and salt.

Nutrition Information

- Calories: 151 calories;
- Total Carbohydrate: 22.5
- Cholesterol: 0
- Protein: 6.4
- Total Fat: 5

- Sodium: 440

15. Creole Okra

Serving: 4 | Prep: 10mins | Ready in:

Ingredients

- 2 tablespoons olive oil
- 1/2 large onion, chopped
- 2 cloves garlic, minced
- 1/2 green bell pepper, chopped
- 1 (16 ounce) can diced tomatoes in juice
- 3/8 teaspoon dried thyme
- 2 tablespoons chopped fresh parsley
- 1/4 teaspoon cayenne pepper
- salt and pepper to taste
- 1 (16 ounce) package frozen cut okra

Direction

- In a large skillet, heat the olive oil over medium heat. Sauté the garlic and the onion until limp. Add the green pepper and stir until tender. Drain the tomatoes. Reserve the juice. Pour them into the skillet. Season it with pepper, salt, cayenne, parsley and thyme. Simmer over medium heat for 5 minutes.
- Add the frozen okra. Cover the bottom of the pan with enough reserved juice from the tomatoes. Cover the pan. Cook until okra is tender or for 15 minutes.

Nutrition Information

- Calories: 133 calories;
- Sodium: 184
- Total Carbohydrate: 14.2
- Cholesterol: 0
- Protein: 4
- Total Fat: 7.2

16. Crispy Fried Okra Salad

Serving: 6 | Prep: 15mins | Ready in:

Ingredients

- 1 pound bacon
- 1 (24 ounce) bag frozen breaded okra
- 3 large tomatoes, diced
- 1 red onion, diced
- 1 pinch garlic salt to taste
- salt and ground black pepper to taste

Direction

- In a large skillet put the bacon. Cook it for about 10 minutes over medium-high heat until it turns brown evenly. Turn occasionally in between. Using paper towels to drain the bacon slices. In a large bowl, crumble the bacon.
- In a large saucepan or a deep-fryer heat 1/2 inch of the vegetable oil over 175°C or 350°F. For 3 to 4 minutes, fry the okra in the hot oil until it turns golden brown. Turn often in between. Using paper towels drain it. Add the bacon into the bowl.
- In a separate bowl, toss the pepper, salt, garlic salt, red onion and tomatoes together. Mix in the okra mixture and the bacon together.

Nutrition Information

- Calories: 374 calories;
- Total Fat: 26
- Sodium: 810
- Total Carbohydrate: 23.5
- Cholesterol: 30
- Protein: 13.1

17. Dinengdeng

Serving: 6 | Prep: 30mins | Ready in:

Ingredients

- 2 (8 ounce) fillets milkfish (bangus)
- 1 tomato, quartered
- 1 onion, chopped
- 2 tablespoons shrimp paste (bagoong)
- 1 cup water
- salt and pepper to taste
- 1/2 pound long beans, cut into bite-size pieces
- 1/2 pound zucchini, cut into bite-size pieces
- 1/2 pound fresh okra

Direction

- Prepare an outdoor grill by preheating to medium heat and lightly oil the grate.
- Place the milkfish fillet on the griller then grill for 2 to 3 minutes each side, until the flesh flakes simply with a fork.
- Mix water, shrimp paste, onion, tomato, and grilled fillet to the pot; make it boil for 5 minutes. Add pepper and salt to taste. Add the zucchini and long beans; mix. Then cover the pot and cook for 5 minutes on medium heat. Mix the okra into the mixture and cook for 5 more minutes. Serve right away.

Nutrition Information

- Calories: 288 calories;
- Total Fat: 5.8
- Sodium: 101
- Total Carbohydrate: 32.7
- Cholesterol: 43
- Protein: 27.5

18. Dixie Pork Stir Fry

Serving: 4 | Prep: 10mins | Ready in:

Ingredients

- 1 tablespoon oil

- 1 Smithfield® Portobello Mushroom Marinated Fresh Pork Loin Filet, cut into thin strips
- 1 teaspoon dried thyme leaves
- 1/2 teaspoon minced garlic
- 1 medium sweet yellow onion, thinly sliced
- 1 medium red bell pepper, thinly sliced
- 1 (10 ounce) package frozen baby cob corn, thawed and drained
- 1 (10 ounce) package frozen sliced okra, thawed and drained
- 2 tablespoons chopped fresh parsley
- Hot pepper sauce (optional)

Direction

- In a big skillet, heat oil over medium-high heat. Stir-fry the garlic, thyme and the pork strips. Stir-fry until pork turns brown in color.
- Put the okra, corn, red pepper and the onion. Stir-fry until the onion is crisp-tender.
- Mix the parsley. Add hot sauce if desired.

Nutrition Information

- Calories: 375 calories;
- Sodium: 460
- Total Carbohydrate: 29.6
- Cholesterol: 85
- Protein: 36.6
- Total Fat: 14.4

19. Easy Creole Okra And Shrimp

Serving: 8 | Prep: 20mins | Ready in:

Ingredients

- 2 tablespoons olive oil
- 1 green bell pepper, chopped
- 1 small onion, chopped
- 2 (14.5 ounce) cans diced tomatoes
- 3 cooked andouille sausage, cut into quarters
- 1 (10 ounce) package frozen cut okra, thawed

- 2 tablespoons Cajun seasoning, or to taste
- 2 teaspoons salt
- 2 pounds peeled and deveined medium shrimp (30-40 per pound)

Direction

- Heat olive oil in skillet on medium heat. Mix onion and bell pepper in; mix and cook for about 5 minutes till onion is translucent and soft. Mix tomatoes in. Simmer for 10 minutes. Add salt, Cajun seasoning, sausage and okra. Cover. Cook for 30 minutes. Mix shrimp in; cook for 8-12 minutes till meat isn't transparent in the middle and bright pink outside.

Nutrition Information

- Calories: 205 calories;
- Total Fat: 7
- Sodium: 1163
- Total Carbohydrate: 10
- Cholesterol: 175
- Protein: 25.5

20. Easy Indian Style Okra

Serving: 4 | Prep: 10mins | Ready in:

Ingredients

- 3 tablespoons butter
- 1 medium onion, chopped
- 1 pound sliced fresh okra
- 1/2 teaspoon ground cumin
- 1/2 teaspoon ground ginger
- 1/2 teaspoon ground coriander
- 1/4 teaspoon ground black pepper
- salt to taste

Direction

- In a big skillet, melt butter over medium heat. Add the onion. Cook until it is tender. Mix the okra. Add the salt, pepper, coriander, ginger and the cumin to season. Sauté for a few minutes. Turn the heat to medium-low. Cover the pan and cook for 20 minutes. Stir it occasionally until the okra is tender.

Nutrition Information

- Calories: 126 calories;
- Total Fat: 8.9
- Sodium: 72
- Total Carbohydrate: 11.1
- Cholesterol: 23
- Protein: 2.8

21. Egyptian Bamia

Serving: 4 | Prep: 15mins | Ready in:

Ingredients

- 1/4 cup olive oil
- 1 large onion, finely chopped
- 1 pound boneless lamb shoulder, cut into 1-inch pieces
- salt and ground black pepper to taste
- 1 (8 ounce) can tomato sauce
- 2 cups water, or as needed to cover
- 1 (10 ounce) package frozen okra, thawed

Direction

- In big saucepan, heat olive oil on medium heat; mix and cook for about 7 minutes till onion is translucent. Mix black pepper, salt and lamb in. Mix and cook for 5-10 minutes more till lamb is lightly browned.
- Mix water and tomato sauce in; season with black pepper and salt. Boil lamb mixture; lower heat to low. Simmer lamb in the sauce for minimum of 1 hour till very tender; add more water if needed. Occasionally mix.
- Preheat an oven to 175°C/350°F.

- Mix okra in lamb mixture, adding extra water if needed; boil. Spoon bamia into 2-qt. baking dish. Adjust black pepper and salt. Use foil to cover dish.
- In preheated oven, bake for about 45 minutes till okra is tender. Uncover at final 10 minutes of baking.

Nutrition Information

- Calories: 339 calories;
- Total Fat: 25.7
- Sodium: 337
- Total Carbohydrate: 11.2
- Cholesterol: 58
- Protein: 16.9

22. Falling In Love With Okra

Serving: 12 | Prep: 20mins | Ready in:

Ingredients

- cooking spray
- 1/4 cup butter, melted
- 1 1/2 pounds okra, cut into 1-inch pieces
- 3 ears fresh corn kernels
- 1 large sweet onion, chopped
- 1 clove garlic, minced
- 1/4 cup half-and-half
- salt and ground black pepper to taste

Direction

- Spray cooking spray on big skillet. Add butter; melt on medium high heat. Add onion, corn and okra; sauté for 3-5 minutes till barely tender. Add garlic; sauté for about 5 more minutes till all veggies are tender. Lower heat; add half and half. Mix to combine. Season with pepper and salt.

Nutrition Information

- Calories: 83 calories;
- Total Fat: 4.8
- Sodium: 51
- Total Carbohydrate: 9.7
- Cholesterol: 12
- Protein: 2.2

23. Fire Roasted Vegetarian Gumbo

Serving: 8 | Prep: 45mins | Ready in:

Ingredients

- 1 serrano pepper
- 1 banana pepper
- 1 small jalapeno chile pepper
- 1/4 cup canola oil
- 1/4 cup all-purpose flour
- 2 tablespoons canola oil
- 2 celery ribs, chopped
- 1 large onion, chopped
- 3 green bell peppers, chopped
- 1 quart vegetable broth
- 2 cloves garlic, minced
- 2 tablespoons Cajun seasoning
- 1 tablespoon smoked paprika
- 1 tablespoon file powder
- 1 cup fire-roasted tomatoes
- 1 sweet potato, peeled and cubed
- parsnip, peeled and cubed
- 1 cup canned red beans, rinsed and drained
- 1 cup canned black-eyed peas, rinsed and drained
- 2 cups frozen cut okra, thawed

Direction

- Preheat an oven to broil.
- On baking sheet, put jalapeno chile peppers, banana and serrano; put in oven. Broil, watching carefully, for 4-5 minutes till skins blister and blacken. Flip peppers. Broil till all sides blacken. Take peppers out of oven. Put into sealed paper bag to let steam. Remove peppers from bag after 15-20 minutes. Peel crispy black skin off. Remove seeds and stems from peppers and chop coarsely. Put into bowl.
- Heat canola oil in big skillet on medium heat till a sprinkled pinch of flour on oil starts to bubble. Whisk leftover flour in. Cook, continuously whisking, for about 20 minutes till mixture is dark brown and well blended. Take roux off heat when it's dark brown.
- Heat 2 tbsp. canola oil in deep soup pot on medium high heat. Mix 1/2 bell peppers and onions and celery in when oil starts to smoke. Mix and cook for about 5 minutes till onion is transparent and veggies are tender. Mix 1/4 cup vegetable broth into pot; cover. Simmer for 10-15 minutes till nearly all liquid evaporates.
- Mix uncooked onions and bell peppers, jalapeno chile peppers, banana, serrano, smoked paprika file powder, Cajun seasoning, garlic into cooked onions and bell peppers. Mix 1 cup stock and roux into veggie mixture till roux melts. Cover. Simmer for 5 minutes. Add leftover stock, okra, black-eyed peas, red beans, parsnip, sweet potato and tomatoes. Simmer for 30 more minutes, uncovered. Season with pepper and salt to taste.

Nutrition Information

- Calories: 268 calories;
- Total Fat: 11.8
- Sodium: 886
- Total Carbohydrate: 35.7
- Cholesterol: 0
- Protein: 6.8

24. Fried Okra

Serving: 4 | Prep: 15mins | Ready in:

Ingredients

- 10 pods okra, sliced in 1/4 inch pieces

- 1 egg, beaten
- 1 cup cornmeal
- 1/4 teaspoon salt
- 1/4 teaspoon ground black pepper
- 1/2 cup vegetable oil

Direction

- For 5 to 10 minutes, soak the okra in egg in a small bowl. Combine pepper, salt and the cornmeal in a medium bowl.
- In a large skillet, heat oil over medium-high heat. Coat the okra evenly by dredging it in the cornmeal mixture. In hot oil put the okra carefully; continuously stirring. Turn the heat to medium once the okra starts to turn brown. Cook until it turns golden. Using paper towel, drain the okra.

Nutrition Information

- Calories: 394 calories;
- Sodium: 167
- Total Carbohydrate: 29
- Cholesterol: 46
- Protein: 4.7
- Total Fat: 29.2

25. Fried Okra Salad

Serving: 6 | Prep: 20mins | Ready in:

Ingredients

- 2 slices bacon (optional)
- 2 (10 ounce) packages breaded frozen okra
- 1/3 cup chopped tomato
- 2 tablespoons chopped green onion
- 2 tablespoons chopped green bell pepper
- 1/2 cup vegetable oil
- 1/2 cup white sugar
- 1/4 cup distilled white vinegar

Direction

- In a large skillet, cook the bacon over medium-high heat. Turn it occasionally for about 10 minutes until it turns brown evenly. On paper towels, drain the bacon slices.
- In the same skillet, stir and cook the okra for 10 to 15 minutes or until tender and turns brown in color. Transfer and drain it over paper towels.
- In a bowl, mix the green bell pepper, green onion, tomato, okra and bacon.
- In a microwave-safe bowl, whisk the vinegar, sugar and oil together. For 1 minute, heat it in the microwave on high heat. Stir it every 10 seconds until the sugar is dissolved and the dressing is boiling. Pour over the vegetables. Serve. Toss to coat.

Nutrition Information

- Calories: 267 calories;
- Sodium: 76
- Total Carbohydrate: 22.1
- Cholesterol: 3
- Protein: 3.2
- Total Fat: 19.7

26. Frying Pan Okra

Serving: 8 | Prep: 5mins | Ready in:

Ingredients

- 1 tablespoon butter
- 3 onions, sliced
- 1 pound fresh okra, sliced in 1/8 inch pieces
- 1 1/2 teaspoons ground turmeric

Direction

- In a medium saucepan, melt the butter over medium heat. Sauté the onion until it becomes translucent. Mix the turmeric and the okra. Turn the heat to low and cook until tender, or for 15 minutes.

Nutrition Information

- Calories: 44 calories;
- Total Carbohydrate: 6.6
- Cholesterol: 4
- Protein: 1.7
- Total Fat: 1.7
- Sodium: 15

27. Grandma Oma's Pickled Okra

Serving: 24 | Prep: 1hours | Ready in:

Ingredients

- 1 1/2 pounds fresh okra
- 3 dried red chile peppers
- 3 teaspoons dried dill
- 2 cups water
- 1 cup vinegar
- 2 tablespoons salt

Direction

- Evenly divide fresh okra to 3 1-pint sterile jars. IN each jar, put 1 tsp. dill and 1 dried chile.
- Mix salt, vinegar and water in small saucepan; put on rolling boil. Put over ingredients in jars. Seal for 10 minutes in hot water bath. Before opening, refrigerate jars.

Nutrition Information

- Calories: 10 calories;
- Cholesterol: 0
- Protein: 0.6
- Total Fat: 0
- Sodium: 585
- Total Carbohydrate: 2.1

28. Grilled Okra

Serving: 4 | Prep: 5mins | Ready in:

Ingredients

- 1 pound fresh okra
- 1/4 cup melted butter
- 1/4 cup Cajun seasoning

Direction

- Preheat the outdoor grill to high heat. Oil the grate lightly.
- In the melted butter, roll the okra. Roll it in the Cajun seasoning after. For about 2 minutes each side, grill the okra until charred.

Nutrition Information

- Calories: 156 calories;
- Total Carbohydrate: 11.4
- Cholesterol: 31
- Protein: 3
- Total Fat: 12
- Sodium: 1501

29. Grilled Okra Salad

Serving: 2 | Prep: 10mins | Ready in:

Ingredients

- 1/4 cup white wine vinegar
- 1 orange tomato, cubed
- 1/2 red onion, diced
- salt to taste
- 16 pods fresh okra

Direction

- Preheat outdoor grill to medium high heat; oil grate lightly. Mix salt, onion, tomato and vinegar in a bowl; put aside.

- On preheated grill, cook okra for about 5 minutes till several black areas develop on skin. Toss okra with tomato mixture; serve.

Nutrition Information

- Calories: 50 calories;
- Total Fat: 0.2
- Sodium: 35
- Total Carbohydrate: 11
- Cholesterol: 0
- Protein: 2.9

30. Guinean Okra Sauce

Serving: 8 | Prep: 5mins | Ready in:

Ingredients

- 1/2 pound frozen whole okra
- 1 serrano pepper, chopped
- 2 cloves garlic, roughly chopped
- 1 tablespoon lemon juice
- 1/2 teaspoon salt

Direction

- Put a big pot of water to a rolling boil on high heat. Mix frozen okra in when water boils; boil again. Cook okra for about 8 minutes, uncovered. In colander set in sink; drain well. Don't rinse. Trim okra stems off.
- In a food processor, process salt, lemon juice, garlic, chile pepper and trimmed okra for about 30 seconds till smooth. Season to taste.

Nutrition Information

- Calories: 10 calories;
- Sodium: 146
- Total Carbohydrate: 2.3
- Cholesterol: 0
- Protein: 0.5
- Total Fat: 0.1

31. Hearty Creole Okra And Tomatoes

Serving: 12 | Prep: 20mins | Ready in:

Ingredients

- 2 tablespoons butter
- 2 tablespoons olive oil
- 4 stalks celery, chopped
- 2 onions, chopped
- 4 ears fresh corn, shucked and kernels scraped from cob
- 2 pounds fresh okra, cut into 1/2 inch slices
- 2 (28 ounce) cans whole tomatoes, broken up
- 1/2 pound andouille sausage, diced
- 1/2 teaspoon Creole seasoning, or to taste
- sea salt and ground black pepper to taste

Direction

- In a big pot, heat olive oil and butter over medium heat. Cook for about 5 minutes, stirring in the onions and the celery, until the onions are translucent. Add the corn kernels. Cook for 3 minutes.
- Mix the Creole seasoning, andouille sausage, tomatoes and okra in. Cover. Cook for at least 45 minutes over medium heat until the okra has lost all its slippery texture. Season it with more Creole seasoning if necessary, black pepper and sea salt. Cook for about 10 minutes uncovered to reduce the liquid.

Nutrition Information

- Calories: 180 calories;
- Total Fat: 10.4
- Sodium: 436
- Total Carbohydrate: 19.1
- Cholesterol: 16
- Protein: 6.2

32. Husband's Grandmother's Shrimp Gumbo

Serving: 12 | Prep: 45mins | Ready in:

Ingredients

- 1 pound smoked sausage links, cut into 1/4-inch slices
- 1/4 pound bacon, chopped
- 2 cups chopped okra
- 1 (14.5 ounce) can diced tomatoes with green chile peppers
- 1/2 cup unsalted butter
- 2/3 cup all-purpose flour
- 2 cups chopped onion
- 1/2 cup chopped green onions
- 2/3 cup finely chopped green bell pepper
- 2/3 cup finely chopped celery
- 2 tablespoons chopped fresh parsley
- 2 tablespoons minced garlic
- 2 cups water
- salt to taste
- ground black pepper to taste
- 1/4 teaspoon cayenne pepper
- 1 teaspoon dried thyme
- 2 bay leaves
- 6 cups water
- 2 pounds uncooked medium shrimp, peeled and deveined

Direction

- Brown sausage in skillet on medium heat; discard fat in skillet. Drain sausage slices over paper towels so it absorbs extra grease. Put aside sausage. Mix and cook chopped bacon in skillet for 6-8 minutes till crisp. Remove bacon; put aside. Mix okra into hot bacon drippings; mix and cook for about 5 minutes till okra is tender. In colander, drain okra. Discard the bacon drippings.
- Put diced tomatoes and okra in saucepan on medium heat; simmer. Lower heat to medium low. Simmer okra mixture for about 10 minutes.
- Melt butter in big soup pot on medium heat; mix and cook garlic, parsley, celery, green pepper, green onions and onion for about 10 minutes till onion starts to brown. Remove veggies; leave butter in pot. Mix flour in; lower heat to low. Cook roux, constantly mixing, for 30-45 minutes till the color is like milk chocolate. Don't burn roux.
- Whisk 2 cups water in when roux reaches proper color. Bring heat to medium; mix bay leaves, thyme, cayenne pepper, pepper and salt in. Boil mixture. Mix 6 cups more water, okra-tomato mixture, bacon and sausage in. Lower heat to medium low. Simmer gumbo, occasionally mixing, for about 45 minutes till flavors merge and soup is thick. Mix shrimp in; simmer for 6-8 minutes more till opaque and pink. Discard bay leaves and if desired, adjust seasonings. Serve.

Nutrition Information

- Calories: 343 calories;
- Protein: 23.9
- Total Fat: 21.8
- Sodium: 922
- Total Carbohydrate: 12.6
- Cholesterol: 165

33. Indian Chickpea Stir Fry

Serving: 4 | Prep: 20mins | Ready in:

Ingredients

- 1 russet potato
- 2 teaspoons vegetable oil, or to taste
- 1/2 yellow onion, thinly sliced
- 1 teaspoon ground turmeric
- 2 teaspoons curry powder
- 1 teaspoon monosodium glutamate (MSG)
- 1 (15 ounce) can chickpeas, drained

- 1 pinch chili powder, or to taste
- 1 cup okra
- 1 teaspoon sumac powder
- 2 teaspoons tamarind paste
- 6 Thai chiles, split lengthwise

Direction

- In a small saucepan, cover russet potato with cold water. Boil. Lower heat then simmer for 10 minutes until potato is fork tender. Drain. Cool for 10 minutes until safe to handle. Dice the potato.
- In a skillet, heat vegetable oil on medium heat. Stir and cook turmeric and onion for 5 minutes until onion becomes soft. Add monosodium glutamate and curry powder. Mix in chili powder and chickpeas. Stir in and cook okra for 5-7 minutes until soft. Stir in sumac and diced potato to coat. Mix in chiles and tamarind paste.

Nutrition Information

- Calories: 190 calories;
- Total Fat: 3.4
- Sodium: 343
- Total Carbohydrate: 34.8
- Cholesterol: 0
- Protein: 5.7

34. Instant Pot® Brunswick Stew

Serving: 6 | Prep: 10mins | Ready in:

Ingredients

- 2 (14.5 ounce) cans whole peeled tomatoes
- 2 russet potatoes, peeled and diced, or more to taste
- 2 cups chicken broth
- 1 cup diced onion
- 1/4 cup Worcestershire sauce
- 1/4 cup apple cider vinegar

- 3 tablespoons ketchup
- 1/2 teaspoon red pepper flakes, or to taste
- 2 (6 ounce) bone-in chicken breast halves
- 1/4 teaspoon seasoned salt, or to taste
- 1 dash ground thyme
- ground black pepper to taste
- 1 (10 ounce) package frozen corn
- 1 (10 ounce) package frozen baby lima beans
- 1 (10 ounce) package frozen sliced okra
- 3/4 cup shredded cooked pork, or to taste

Direction

- In a multi-functional cooker like Instant Pot®, mix together red pepper flakes, tomatoes, ketchup, potatoes, vinegar, chicken broth, Worcestershire sauce, and onion. Place the chicken breast on top; put black pepper, thyme, and seasoned salt. Secure lid and put on high pressure for 20 minutes to set on timer following the cooker's manual. Let the pressure build for 10-15 minutes.
- Use the quick-release method to relieve steam carefully for 5 minutes in accordance with the cooker's manual. Unlock and remove lid.
- Move the chicken on a plate; let it cool. Add okra, lima beans, and corn in the pot; mix well.
- Remove skin from the chicken, shred the meat off the bones return the meat in the pot; place pork. Secure lid and put on low pressure, cook for 15 minutes until the veggies are heated through. Use the quick-release method in relieving pressure carefully for 5 minutes in accordance with the cooker's manual. Unlock and remove lid.

Nutrition Information

- Calories: 312 calories;
- Total Fat: 4.7
- Sodium: 941
- Total Carbohydrate: 44.8
- Cholesterol: 49
- Protein: 24

35. Island Okras

Serving: 6 | Prep: 10mins | Ready in:

Ingredients

- 3 tablespoons olive oil
- 1 large onion, thinly sliced
- 2 cloves garlic, minced
- 4 cups fresh okra, ends trimmed and halved lengthwise
- salt to taste
- ground black pepper to taste
- 1 lime, juiced

Direction

- In a skillet, heat the olive oil over medium heat. Mix the garlic and the onion. Stir and cook for about 5 minutes until the onion has turned translucent and has softened.
- Put the pepper, salt and the okra. From medium heat, turn it to high heat. Stir and cook for about 10 minutes until the okra is starting to get brown color. Add the lime juice over the okra. Continue cooking for 2 minutes.

Nutrition Information

- Calories: 96 calories;
- Cholesterol: 0
- Protein: 1.8
- Total Fat: 6.9
- Sodium: 7
- Total Carbohydrate: 8.6

36. Jambo (Dutch Antilles Okra Soup)

Serving: 4 | Prep: 25mins | Ready in:

Ingredients

- 6 ounces salt beef, fat removed and diced
- 12 cups water
- Salt and pepper to taste
- 3 cups fresh okra, cut into 1/2 inch slices
- 1 cup medium shrimp, peeled and deveined
- 8 ounces cod fillets, cubed
- 1/4 cup chopped fresh basil
- 1 tablespoon lemon juice, to taste

Direction

- In ample cool water, soak diced beef to remove salt overnight. Drain then rise; put aside.
- Boil 12 cups water on high heat. Add pepper and salt to taste. Add okra. Lower heat to medium; simmer for 20 minutes. Mix cod, shrimp and beef in; simmer for 10 more minutes. Season with lemon juice and chopped basil; serve.

Nutrition Information

- Calories: 189 calories;
- Total Carbohydrate: 6
- Cholesterol: 96
- Protein: 24.3
- Total Fat: 7.4
- Sodium: 601

37. Japanese Simmered Bottle Gourd, Okra, And Tofu

Serving: 4 | Prep: 15mins | Ready in:

Ingredients

- 1/2 bitter melon, seeded and thinly sliced crosswise
- 2 tablespoons salt
- 14 ounces fried tofu, cut into bite-sized pieces
- 7 ounces bottle gourd, peeled and cut into bite-sized pieces
- 1/2 cup prepared kombu dashi stock
- 1 tablespoon soy sauce
- 1 teaspoon mirin (Japanese sweet wine)

- 8 pods fresh okra, trimmed
- 1 teaspoon grated ginger

Direction

- In a large bowl with water, put bitter melon slices. Add salt and mix until dissolved. For 15 to 20 minutes, soak before draining.
- Mix in a microwave pressure cooker, the bitter tofu, melon and bottle gourd.
- In a small bowl, combine soy sauce, dashi stock, and mirin then put over the bitter melon mixture. Following manufacturers' instructions, close the pressure cooker. Set at 600W power in microwave and cook for 7 minutes.
- Open the pressure cooker and add okra. Close again and cook until okra becomes tender, 1 minute.
- Pour bitter melon mixture on to a serving plate and season with grated ginger.

Nutrition Information

- Calories: 298 calories;
- Protein: 19.1
- Total Fat: 20.3
- Sodium: 3778
- Total Carbohydrate: 15.5
- Cholesterol: 1

38. Kadai Bhindi (Indian Style Okra With Bell Peppers)

Serving: 4 | Prep: 15mins | Ready in:

Ingredients

- 1 cup oil for frying, or as needed
- 2 cups okra, cut into bite-size pieces
- 2 tablespoons vegetable oil
- 1 cup diced onion
- 1 teaspoon salt, or to taste
- 1 green chile pepper, chopped

- 1/2 teaspoon ginger paste
- 1/2 teaspoon garlic paste
- 1 pinch ground turmeric
- 1 cup diced fresh tomatoes
- 2 teaspoons ground coriander
- 2 teaspoons ground cumin
- 1/2 teaspoon cayenne powder
- 2 cups chopped bell peppers (yellow, green, red)
- 1 cup chopped fresh cilantro (coriander)
- 1/2 teaspoon garam masala

Direction

- In a skillet, heat about an inch of oil over medium heat. To reduce stickiness of the okra yet maintaining the green color, fry it for 2 to 3 minutes in the hot oil. In a paper towel-lined plate, transfer the fried okra.
- In a separate skillet, heat 2 tablespoons of oil. Add and stir salt and onion. For 5 to 10 minutes, cook until onion is transparent. Add the turmeric, garlic paste, ginger paste and the green chile pepper. Cook for about 1 minute until the onion is coated evenly.
- Add the tomatoes into the seasoned onion mixture. For 2 minutes, let it cook. Put the cayenne powder, ground cumin and the ground coriander. Cook for about 4 minutes. Stir until the tomatoes are cooked but not completely mashed.
- Add the cilantro and the bell peppers in the onion-tomato mixture. For 2 minutes, cook and stir it. Add the okra. For 4 minutes, cook it over very low heat. Sprinkle the garam masala over.

Nutrition Information

- Calories: 186 calories;
- Sodium: 622
- Total Carbohydrate: 15.9
- Cholesterol: 0
- Protein: 3.4
- Total Fat: 13.3

39. Kentucky Burgoo

Serving: 20 | Prep: 1hours10mins | Ready in:

Ingredients

- 5 pounds bone-in mutton shoulder or leg, cut into 1 pound pieces
- 2 teaspoons salt
- 1 tablespoon Italian seasoning
- 3 pounds baking potatoes, peeled and cubed
- 1 pound carrots, peeled and sliced
- 2 (15 ounce) cans crushed tomatoes
- 2 teaspoons extra-virgin olive oil or canola oil
- 1 small onion, chopped
- 2 cups medium salsa
- 1 (15 ounce) can tomato sauce
- 1/2 cup packed brown sugar
- 1/4 cup hickory smoke flavored barbeque sauce
- 1 (15.25 ounce) can whole kernel corn, drained
- 1 (14.5 ounce) can green beans, drained
- 1 (16 ounce) package frozen lima beans, thawed
- 1 (10 ounce) package frozen okra
- 1 (46 fluid ounce) can tomato juice

Direction

- Day 1: Place meat in a big heavy pot, add water to. Add 1tsp salt, Italian seasoning, and water to cover the meat. Let it simmer for an hour over medium heat.
- Turn on the oven to 190°C (375°F) to preheat. Take the meat out of stock. Place the stock inside the fridge for later use. Separate the bones from the meat, throw out bones, and put the meat inside a roasting pan. Let it roast in heated oven for 1 1/2 hour or until when poked with a fork it is tender. Using an aluminum foil, cover the pan and place it inside the fridge.
- Day 2: Take out stock from the fridge, skim off the thickened white fat on the top and discard it. In a heavy stock pot, pour in 4 cups of stock and add 1 can crushed tomatoes, carrots,

potatoes, and 1 tsp salt. Let it cook for 20 minutes over medium-high heat, stirring from time to time. Let it cool for a little and then refrigerate.

- Preheat oven to 150°C or 300°F. In a small frying pan, heat olive oil over medium heat and add onion. Cook the onion and stir until translucent, 5-8 minutes. Put to the side. Take the meat out of fridge and add the rest of the stock to the pan. Place a lid or some aluminum foil on the roasting pan.
- Place the meat in heated oven for 1 1/2 hours to cook. Take the meat out of oven and pour in tomato sauce, salsa, 1 can crushed tomatoes, brown sugar, onion, and barbecue sauce. Proceed with roasting for an additional 1 1/2 hours. Let it cool a little and place it inside the fridge overnight.
- Day 3: In a big stock pot or Dutch oven portable roaster, combine the vegetable mixture from day 2 with the meat, green beans, corns, lima beans, tomato juice, and okra. Cook at 150°C (or 300°F) if using a roaster or simmer, if a stock pot is being used, over medium-low heat, stirring from time to time.

Nutrition Information

- Calories: 532 calories;
- Total Carbohydrate: 49.7
- Cholesterol: 82
- Protein: 28.2
- Total Fat: 25.6
- Sodium: 975

40. Kingombo Patatas

Serving: 8 | Prep: 15mins | Ready in:

Ingredients

- 1/2 cup cornmeal
- salt and ground black pepper to taste

- 2 large potatoes, cut into 1/2-inch cubes
- 1 pound fresh okra, trimmed and cut into 1/2-inch pieces
- 1 white onion, finely chopped
- 1/2 cup cooking oil

Direction

- In a large resealabe plastic bag, mix the pepper, salt and cornmeal together. Put the onion, okra and the potatoes. Seal the bag. Coat the vegetables with the cornmeal mixture by shaking it well.
- In a big skillet, heat the cooking oil over medium heat. Let it simmer but do not let it smoke. Put the vegetables in. For 10 to 12 minutes, cook in the hot oil until the okra and onion turn brown and the potatoes are tender. Use a slotted spoon to move the cooked vegetable to the paper towel-lined plate.

Nutrition Information

- Calories: 133 calories;
- Total Fat: 1.7
- Sodium: 30
- Total Carbohydrate: 26.9
- Cholesterol: 0
- Protein: 3.6

41. Lamb And Okra Stew

Serving: 6 | Prep: 20mins | Ready in:

Ingredients

- 2 tablespoons extra-virgin olive oil
- 1/4 cup crushed garlic
- 2 pounds cubed leg of lamb meat
- 1 teaspoon ground cumin
- 1 teaspoon chopped fresh mint
- 1 teaspoon ground dried turmeric
- 1 teaspoon chopped fresh rosemary
- 2 (14.5 ounce) cans diced tomatoes, drained

- 2 tablespoons tomato paste
- 1 pound baby okra
- 1 teaspoon lemon juice
- 1 cup water
- 1 tablespoon butter
- 1 cup thin egg noodles
- 2 cups long grain rice
- 2 cups chicken broth
- 2 cups water
- 1 pinch salt and pepper to taste
- 1 teaspoon olive oil

Direction

- In a big skillet, heat olive oil over medium heat. Cook the garlic until it turns transparent. Put the cubed lamb. Cook it until all of its side turns brown. Season it with rosemary, turmeric, mint and cumin. Let it cook for another 5 minutes. Put the okra, tomato paste and the diced tomatoes. Stir the mixture of the water and the lemon juice in the skillet. Cover it and for 45 minutes, let it simmer over low heat.
- In a saucepan, melt the butter over medium heat. Put the egg noodles. Sauté until it is toasted. Put the water and the chicken broth. Bring it to a boil. Mix the rice in. For about 15 minutes, cover and let simmer until the rice is tender over low heat. Season it with pepper and salt. Mix olive oil in. Top the lamb stew on the rice pilaf and serve.

Nutrition Information

- Calories: 552 calories;
- Total Fat: 19.1
- Sodium: 325
- Total Carbohydrate: 67
- Cholesterol: 72
- Protein: 25.5

42. Lemony Grilled Okra

Serving: 6 | Prep: 10mins | Ready in:

Ingredients

- 1 pound okra, stems trimmed
- 1 tablespoon extra-virgin olive oil, or more as needed
- 1 pinch paprika, or to taste
- 1 pinch garlic powder, or to taste
- salt and freshly ground black pepper to taste
- 1 pinch cayenne pepper
- 1 lemon, juiced
- 1/4 teaspoon chopped fresh rosemary, or to taste
- 1/4 teaspoon chopped fresh thyme, or to taste

Direction

- Preheat outdoor grill to high heat; oil the grate lightly.
- In a bowl, toss cayenne pepper, pepper, salt, garlic powder, paprika, olive oil and okra.
- On preheated grill, grill okra for 5 minutes till 1 side has visible grill marks and until it turns to bright green. Flip the okra and cover the grill. Cook for 5 minutes till tender.
- Put okra into a serving bowl. Sprinkle thyme, rosemary and lemon juice.

Nutrition Information

- Calories: 45 calories;
- Sodium: 32
- Total Carbohydrate: 5.6
- Cholesterol: 0
- Protein: 1.6
- Total Fat: 2.4

43. Okra Curry

Serving: 4 | Prep: 5mins | Ready in:

Ingredients

- 1 pound okra, ends trimmed, cut into 1/4-inch rounds
- 1 tablespoon olive oil
- 1 teaspoon whole cumin seeds
- 1/2 teaspoon curry powder
- 1/2 teaspoon chickpea flour
- 1/2 teaspoon salt

Direction

- Microwave okra for 3 minutes on high.
- In big skillet, heat olive oil on medium heat then add cumin. When it's golden brown and swells, mix okra in. Mix and cook for 5 minutes on medium heat. Mix salt, chickpea flour and curry powder in gently; cook for 2 more minutes. Immediately serve.

Nutrition Information

- Calories: 69 calories;
- Sodium: 301
- Total Carbohydrate: 8.5
- Cholesterol: 0
- Protein: 2.4
- Total Fat: 3.7

44. Okra Fritters

Serving: 6 | Prep: 15mins | Ready in:

Ingredients

- 2 pounds fresh okra, sliced in 1/8 inch pieces
- 1 large tomato, diced
- 1 onion, diced
- 6 packets instant grits
- 2 eggs, lightly beaten
- salt and black pepper to taste
- 1/2 cup oil for frying, or as needed

Direction

- In a big bowl, mix onion, tomato and okra. Add pepper, salt, eggs and grids; use your hands to blend.
- In cast iron skillet, heat oil on medium high heat. Shape patties to 2 1/2-in. in diameter, about 1/2 size of a hamburger. Put fritter in pan; cook for about 5 minutes till golden brown.
- Use a spatula to flip; cook for 5 more minutes till other side is browned. Transfer to paper towels; drain. Immediately serve.

Nutrition Information

- Calories: 196 calories;
- Cholesterol: 62
- Protein: 8
- Total Fat: 4
- Sodium: 343
- Total Carbohydrate: 35.7

45. Okra Fry

Serving: 2 | Prep: | Ready in:

Ingredients

- 1 pound fresh okra
- salt to taste
- 2 teaspoons chili powder
- 3 tablespoons olive oil
- 1 pinch asafoetida powder
- 1/2 teaspoon brown mustard seeds

Direction

- Rinse the okra. Cut its tail and head one by one. Chop it to small pieces.
- Combine the asafoetida powder, chili powder, salt and okra in a small mixing bowl.
- Heat the oil over medium-high heat in a medium size skillet. Put the black mustard seeds. Cook until seeds pop. Put the mixture

of okra to the skillet. Cover. For 10 to 15 minutes, let it fry. Serve while hot.

Nutrition Information

- Calories: 262 calories;
- Sodium: 45
- Total Carbohydrate: 18
- Cholesterol: 0
- Protein: 5.1
- Total Fat: 21.1

46. Okra Gumbo

Serving: 8 | Prep: 15mins | Ready in:

Ingredients

- 1 tablespoon vegetable oil
- 1 clove garlic, minced
- 1 medium onion, finely chopped
- 1 medium green bell pepper, finely chopped
- 1/2 (16 ounce) package frozen okra, thawed and sliced
- 8 ounces fresh mushrooms, sliced
- 1 (14.5 ounce) can diced tomatoes with juice
- 1 (6 ounce) can tomato paste
- 1/2 teaspoon file powder
- 2 bay leaves
- 1 teaspoon salt
- 1 teaspoon ground black pepper
- 2 tablespoons vegetable oil
- 2 tablespoons all-purpose flour

Direction

- In a big saucepan, heat 1 tablespoon of oil over medium heat. Mix in the green bell pepper, onion and the garlic. Sauté until tender. Mix in the pepper, salt, bay leaves, file powder, tomato paste, diced tomatoes and their liquid, mushrooms and the okra. Cook for 40 minutes. Stir occasionally in between.

- In a medium skillet, heat 2 tablespoons of oil over medium heat. Stir constantly in between. Add the flour. Cook until a golden brown roux has formed for 2 to 5 minutes.
- Mix the roux into the okra mixture. Continue to cook for the next 5 to 10 minutes until it thickens. Stir occasionally in between.

Nutrition Information

- Calories: 105 calories;
- Protein: 3.2
- Total Fat: 5.5
- Sodium: 542
- Total Carbohydrate: 12.4
- Cholesterol: 0

47. Okra Patties

Serving: 6 | Prep: 20mins | Ready in:

Ingredients

- 3 cups vegetable oil for frying
- 1 pound okra, finely chopped
- 1 cup finely chopped onion
- 1 teaspoon salt
- 1/4 teaspoon pepper
- 1/2 cup water
- 1 egg
- 1/2 cup all-purpose flour
- 1 teaspoon baking powder
- 1/2 cup cornmeal

Direction

- In a large skillet, heat 1 inch of oil over 190 °C or 375 °F.
- Mix the egg, water, pepper, salt, onion and the okra together in a big bowl. Mix the cornmeal, baking powder and the flour. Stir it into the mixture with the okra.
- In the hot oil, carefully drop spoonfuls of the okra batter. For about 2 minutes each side, fry

it until it turns golden. Using the slotted spoon, remove from the skillet and use paper towels to drain it.

Nutrition Information

- Calories: 224 calories;
- Total Fat: 12.3
- Sodium: 467
- Total Carbohydrate: 25.1
- Cholesterol: 31
- Protein: 4.8

48. Okra Rice

Serving: 6 | Prep: 15mins | Ready in:

Ingredients

- 1 pound bacon - cooked and crumbled
- 1 large onion, chopped
- 3 cups sliced fresh or frozen okra
- 1 (14.5 ounce) can chicken broth
- 1 cup uncooked rice
- 1 1/2 cups water

Direction

- In a big, deep skillet, put the bacon. Over medium-high heat, let it cook until it turns brown evenly. Drain the grease. Set it aside for later. Crumble the bacon. Set it aside.
- For about 3 minutes, sauté the onion in a small amount of the reserved bacon grease over medium-high heat until tender using the same skillet. Put the chicken broth, sliced okra and crumbled bacon. Reduce the heat. For about 15 minutes, simmer until the okra is falling apart and tender. Stir in water and rice. Cover. For 20 minutes, simmer or until fluffy.

Nutrition Information

- Calories: 281 calories;

- Total Fat: 10.8
- Sodium: 583
- Total Carbohydrate: 32.3
- Cholesterol: 27
- Protein: 13

49. Okra Salad

Serving: 6 | Prep: 15mins | Ready in:

Ingredients

- 3 slices bacon
- 1 (16 ounce) package frozen cut okra
- 1 onion, chopped
- 1 green bell pepper, seeded and diced
- 1 medium tomato, diced
- 1/3 cup white sugar
- 1/4 cup corn oil
- 1/4 cup white vinegar

Direction

- In a big skillet, put the bacon over medium heat. Cook until it turns brown evenly. Once done, remove and put it on paper towels to drain. On the same pan, just leave a thin coat of oil by removing most of the bacon grease. For about 5 minutes, fry the okra in the same skillet until it is tender. Once done, put the okra in a salad bowl. Toss the tomato, green pepper and the onion. Crumble the bacon in.
- Whisk the vinegar, corn oil and sugar together in a small bowl. Mix until the sugar has dissolved. Put into the salad. Toss to coat. Put it in the fridge for 30 minutes. Serve.

Nutrition Information

- Calories: 226 calories;
- Sodium: 121
- Total Carbohydrate: 19.6
- Cholesterol: 10
- Protein: 3.4

- Total Fat: 15.8

50. Okra Stew With Shrimp

Serving: 4 | Prep: | Ready in:

Ingredients

- 1 pound medium shrimp - peeled and deveined
- 1/2 lime, juiced
- 4 tablespoons margarine
- 2 green bell peppers, seeded
- 6 tablespoons minced shallots
- 1 cup frozen corn kernels
- 1 cup chopped okra
- 3 tomatoes - blanched, peeled and chopped
- 1 tablespoon tomato paste
- 1/4 teaspoon dried thyme
- 1 bay leaf
- salt and pepper to taste
- 1 green chile pepper

Direction

- Put shrimp in a mixing bowl; squeeze lime juice over, evenly trying to coat shrimp.
- Heat butter in stockpot; sauté chives/shallots and green peppers for 2-3 minutes then mix chili pepper, bay leaf, thyme, tomato paste, tomatoes, okra and corn in. Season with pepper and salt; simmer for 10 minutes.
- Add shrimp; boil. Simmer for 5 more minutes. Discard chili and bay leaf; serve.

Nutrition Information

- Calories: 309 calories;
- Total Fat: 13.3
- Sodium: 337
- Total Carbohydrate: 23.1
- Cholesterol: 173
- Protein: 27.1

51. Okra And Tomatoes

Serving: 6 | Prep: 10mins | Ready in:

Ingredients

- 2 slices bacon
- 1 pound frozen okra, thawed and sliced
- 1 small onion, chopped
- 1/2 green bell pepper, chopped
- 2 celery, chopped
- 1 (14.5 ounce) can stewed tomatoes
- salt and pepper to taste

Direction

- In a big, deep skillet, put the bacon in. Over medium-high heat, cook until it turns brown evenly. Once done, drain and crumble the bacon. Set aside.
- Remove the bacon from the pan. In the same pan, sauté the celery, pepper, onion and the okra until tender. Put the pepper, salt and tomatoes. Cook until the tomatoes are heated through.
- If desired, garnish with the crumbled bacon.

Nutrition Information

- Calories: 94 calories;
- Cholesterol: 6
- Protein: 3.8
- Total Fat: 4.7
- Sodium: 250
- Total Carbohydrate: 11.5

52. Okra And Tomatoes II

Serving: 6 | Prep: 15mins | Ready in:

Ingredients

- 1 pound fresh okra

- 1 quart white vinegar
- 3 slices bacon
- 1 large onion, coarsely chopped
- 3 green chile peppers, seeded and chopped
- 5 roma (plum) tomatoes - peeled, seeded and chopped
- salt to taste
- ground black pepper to taste

Direction

- In a bowl, put the okra with the vinegar. Let it soak for 30 minutes. Drain it and rinse. Cut it into 1/2 inch slices.
- In a large, deep skillet, put the bacon. Over medium-high heat, cook until it turns to brown evenly. Drain. Reserve the drippings in the skillet. Cut the bacon into large pieces. Set it aside.
- In the skillet with the bacon drippings, put the green chile peppers and the onion. Over medium heat, cook it for 3 minutes. Mix the tomatoes. Cook for 1 minute. Add the okra and put the bacon back to the skillet. Season it with pepper and salt. To cover, add enough water. Turn the heat to low. Cover the skillet. For 40 minutes, simmer until okra is tender. Serve it while hot.

Nutrition Information

- Calories: 80 calories;
- Total Carbohydrate: 12
- Cholesterol: 5
- Protein: 4.4
- Total Fat: 2.2
- Sodium: 118

53. Okra With Tomatoes

Serving: 6 | Prep: 15mins | Ready in:

Ingredients

- 1 teaspoon olive oil
- 3 cloves garlic, minced
- 1 small onion, minced
- 1 teaspoon cayenne pepper
- 1/2 green bell pepper, minced
- 1 pound frozen sliced okra
- 1 (8 ounce) can canned diced tomatoes
- 1 (15 ounce) can stewed tomatoes
- salt and ground black pepper to taste

Direction

- Over medium heat, put the skillet with the olive oil, enough to cover the bottom of the skillet. Put the cayenne pepper, onion and the garlic. Stir until it is fragrant. Mix the green pepper. For about 5 minutes, stir and cook until it is tender. Mix the frozen okra. Wait for 5 more minutes to allow to cook. Mix the stewed and the diced tomatoes and season with pepper and salt. Turn the heat to medium low. Let it simmer for 5-7 minutes until all the vegetables are tender.

Nutrition Information

- Calories: 66 calories;
- Cholesterol: 0
- Protein: 2.8
- Total Fat: 1.1
- Sodium: 312
- Total Carbohydrate: 13.1

54. Okra, Chicken And Rice Casserole

Serving: 5 | Prep: | Ready in:

Ingredients

- 1 (10.75 ounce) can condensed cream of mushroom soup
- 1 cup water
- 3/4 cup uncooked brown rice

- 1/4 teaspoon paprika
- 1/4 tablespoon ground black pepper
- 4 skinless, boneless chicken breasts
- 1 (16 ounce) package frozen okra, thawed and sliced

Direction

- Preheat oven to 190°C or 375°F.
- Combine the ground black pepper, paprika, okra, rice, water and the soup together in a 9x13 inches baking dish. Put the chicken on top of it. Sprinkle more ground black pepper and paprika.
- Cover. For 45 minutes, in the preheated oven, bake until the juices run clear and until the chicken is cooked through. Increase the water to 1 and 1/3 cups for creamier rice.

Nutrition Information

- Calories: 287 calories;
- Total Carbohydrate: 32
- Cholesterol: 55
- Protein: 26.5
- Total Fat: 5.8
- Sodium: 459

55. Okra, Corn And Tomatoes

Serving: 6 | Prep: | Ready in:

Ingredients

- 2 slices bacon, chopped
- 1 medium onion, chopped
- 1 (10 ounce) package frozen cut okra
- 1 (14.5 ounce) can diced tomatoes, drained
- 1 (20 ounce) package frozen corn
- 1 tablespoon file powder
- salt and pepper to taste

Direction

- In a big skillet on medium high heat, stir and cook bacon to release some juices then add okra and onion. Fry, constantly stir, until browned and tender. This browns quickly, so be careful.
- Put in tomatoes. Simmer for 20 minutes on medium heat. Mix in corn. Simmer for 10 more minutes. Season with pepper, salt and file powder. Serve.

Nutrition Information

- Calories: 167 calories;
- Cholesterol: 6
- Protein: 5.6
- Total Fat: 5.3
- Sodium: 189
- Total Carbohydrate: 27.8

56. Oven Fried Okra

Serving: 4 | Prep: 10mins | Ready in:

Ingredients

- 1 (16 ounce) package frozen cut okra
- butter flavored cooking spray
- 1/4 cup yellow cornmeal
- 1/4 cup panko bread crumbs
- 1/2 teaspoon garlic salt
- 1/4 teaspoon ground black pepper (optional)

Direction

- Preheat oven to 190°C/375°F. Put baking rack over baking sheet/sheet pan.
- In microwave, use your microwave's frozen veggie setting/high to cook frozen okra for 8 minutes; drain. Cool for about 5-10 minutes on paper towels. Generously spray using butter flavored cooking spray. In plastic food storage bag, add pepper, garlic salt, panko breadcrumbs and cornmeal. Put okra into bag; shake to coat okra with cornmeal mixture.

- Take okra from bag; spread on prepped baking rack. In preheated oven, bake for about 15-20 minutes till crispy and golden brown.

Nutrition Information

- Calories: 95 calories;
- Protein: 3.3
- Total Fat: 2
- Sodium: 264
- Total Carbohydrate: 19.1
- Cholesterol: 0

57. Quick And Easy Indian Style Okra

Serving: 6 | Prep: 15mins | Ready in:

Ingredients

- 1/3 cup vegetable oil
- 1/4 teaspoon mustard seed
- 1 pinch asafoetida powder
- 1 medium onion, thinly sliced
- 1 clove garlic, peeled and sliced
- 1/4 teaspoon cumin seed
- 1/8 teaspoon ground turmeric
- 1 large tomato, chopped
- 1 (16 ounce) package frozen sliced okra
- 1/4 teaspoon chili powder
- 1 teaspoon amchoor
- salt to taste

Direction

- In medium skillet, heat oil on medium heat. Cook mustard seed till it starts to crackle. Mix asafetida in. Lower heat to low; mix turmeric, cumin seed, garlic and onion in. Mix and cook for about 5 minutes till onion is tender.
- Mix okra and tomato into mixture. Mix salt, amchoor and chili powder in slowly. Mix and cook till okra is tender yet firm for about 10 minutes.

Nutrition Information

- Calories: 146 calories;
- Cholesterol: 0
- Protein: 1.8
- Total Fat: 12.5
- Sodium: 6
- Total Carbohydrate: 8.6

58. Roasted Okra

Serving: 3 | Prep: 5mins | Ready in:

Ingredients

- 18 fresh okra pods, sliced 1/3 inch thick
- 1 tablespoon olive oil
- 2 teaspoons kosher salt, or to taste
- 2 teaspoons black pepper, or to taste

Direction

- Preheat oven to 220 degrees C/425 degrees F.
- In one layer, put okra slices on a foil-lined cookie sheet. Drizzle olive oil on top. Sprinkle on pepper and salt. Bake for 10-15 minutes in the preheated oven.

Nutrition Information

- Calories: 65 calories;
- Total Fat: 4.6
- Sodium: 1286
- Total Carbohydrate: 5.9
- Cholesterol: 0
- Protein: 1.6

59. Roasted Okra And Cherry Tomatoes

Serving: 6 | Prep: 15mins | Ready in:

Ingredients

- 30 fresh okra, cut into 1-inch pieces, or more to taste
- 6 cherry tomatoes, quartered, or more as desired
- 2 tablespoons extra-virgin olive oil, or as needed
- kosher salt to taste
- 4 slices cooked bacon, crumbled
- 1 teaspoon minced garlic
- 2 tablespoons grated Parmesan cheese, or more to taste

Direction

- Preheat an oven to 175°C/350°F.
- In a bowl, mix tomatoes and okra; drizzle enough olive oil on okra mixture to coat then toss. Season with salt. Mix garlic and bacon into okra mixture; put in baking dish.
- In preheated oven, bake for about 40 minutes till okra is tender. Sprinkle parmesan cheese on okra mixture. Bake for about 5 more minutes till cheese melts.

Nutrition Information

- Calories: 92 calories;
- Total Fat: 6.8
- Sodium: 191
- Total Carbohydrate: 5.2
- Cholesterol: 6
- Protein: 3.5

60. Roux Based Authentic Seafood Gumbo With Okra

Serving: 8 | Prep: 25mins | Ready in:

Ingredients

- Roux:
- 1/2 cup all-purpose flour
- 1/2 cup vegetable oil
- Vegetables:
- 1 tablespoon butter
- 1 cup chopped celery
- 1 cup chopped green onions
- 1 green bell pepper, chopped
- Tomato Sauce and Spices:
- 6 cups water
- 1 (8 ounce) can tomato sauce
- 2 tablespoons Worcestershire sauce
- 2 cloves garlic, minced
- 2 teaspoons salt, or to taste
- 1 teaspoon hot pepper sauce (such as Tabasco®), or to taste
- 1/2 teaspoon dried thyme
- Seafood and Okra:
- 1 pound frozen chopped okra
- 1 pound catfish, cut into 2-inch pieces
- 1 1/2 pounds peeled and deveined shrimp
- Last Addition:
- 1 tablespoon gumbo file powder, or to taste
- 1/2 teaspoon salt, or to taste

Direction

- In big heavy pot/Dutch oven, add flour. Put heat on medium high. Place pot on burner; cook, constantly mixing with a wooden spoon, for about 10 minutes till dark brown, smells like peanuts, bubbly and thick. Put aside to thicken and cool.
- In skillet, melt butter on medium heat. Mix and cook bell pepper, green onions and celery in hot butter for about 10 minutes till tender. Put into pot with roux.
- Mix thyme, hot pepper sauce, 2 tsp. salt, garlic, Worcestershire sauce, tomato sauce and water into veggie mixture. Gently boil mixture. Lower heat to medium low; simmer for an hour.
- Mix okra into veggie mixture; cook for about 15 minutes till tender. Add catfish; gently mix. Cook for about 5 minutes till flesh flakes easily

with a fork. Mix shrimp gently into mixture; cook for about 3 minutes till shrimp are bright pink. Season with salt and file powder; mix.

Nutrition Information

- Calories: 344 calories;
- Total Fat: 20.4
- Sodium: 1129
- Total Carbohydrate: 15.2
- Cholesterol: 159
- Protein: 25.4

61. Shrimp And Okra Gumbo

Serving: 6 | Prep: 15mins | Ready in:

Ingredients

- 2 pounds medium shrimp - peeled and deveined
- salt and pepper to taste
- cayenne pepper to taste
- 1/2 cup olive oil
- 2 pounds chopped okra
- 1 tablespoon tomato paste
- 1 tomato, chopped
- 1 cup chopped onion
- 4 cloves garlic, minced
- 1/2 cup chopped celery
- 1/2 cup chopped green bell pepper
- 12 cups water
- 1/2 cup chopped green onions

Direction

- Season the shrimp to taste with cayenne, pepper and salt. Once done, set it aside. In a big pot, heat the oil over medium heat. Add the okra. For 30 minutes, sauté. Stir occasionally in between. Put the green bell pepper, celery, garlic, onion, tomato and tomato paste. Sauté for 15 more minutes.

- Season to taste by adding the water. Bring to boil. For 45 minutes, simmer over low heat. For 20 minutes more, simmer after adding the shrimp. Put the green onion to the soup. Stir thoroughly.

Nutrition Information

- Calories: 394 calories;
- Protein: 34.8
- Total Fat: 20.9
- Sodium: 270
- Total Carbohydrate: 18.1
- Cholesterol: 230

62. Sinigang Na Bangus (Filipino Milkfish In Tamarind Broth)

Serving: 5 | Prep: 20mins | Ready in:

Ingredients

- 5 cups water
- 2 onions, sliced
- 2 tomatoes, sliced
- 1 pound milkfish (bangus), cut into 5 pieces
- 2 small eggplants, sliced 1/8-inch thick
- 1 cup fresh green beans, cut into 1-inch pieces
- 2 white radishes (labanos), sliced
- 5 pods okra, sliced
- 3 small green chile peppers
- 1 cup watercress (kangkong) leaves and stems
- 1/2 cup tamarind powder
- salt to taste (optional)

Direction

- Add water into a pot. Add tomatoes and onions, and make it boil, covered. Add in green chile peppers, okra, radishes, beans, eggplants, and milkfish. Boil for 5 minutes. Mix in tamarind powder and watercress. Then cover, lower the heat, and add salt to taste. Boil for 5 minutes until the fish is cooked well.

Nutrition Information

- Calories: 291 calories;
- Sodium: 126
- Total Carbohydrate: 38.1
- Cholesterol: 47
- Protein: 23.2
- Total Fat: 6.8

63. Slow Cooker Chicken And Sausage Gumbo

Serving: 6 | Prep: 20mins | Ready in:

Ingredients

- 1/3 cup vegetable oil
- 1/3 cup all-purpose flour
- 3 cups water
- 3/4 pound smoked sausage, quartered lengthwise and sliced
- 1 1/2 cups cubed cooked chicken
- 2 cups sliced okra
- 1 cup chopped onion
- 1/2 cup chopped green bell pepper
- 1/2 cup chopped celery
- 4 cloves garlic, minced
- 1/2 teaspoon salt
- 1/2 teaspoon ground black pepper
- 1/4 teaspoon cayenne pepper

Direction

- Heat vegetable oil in saucepan on medium high heat. Whisk flour in to make a thick paste for about 3 minutes till smooth.
- Lower heat to medium. Cook, constantly whisking, for about 15 minutes till flour is dark reddish-brown roux. Put aside; cool.
- Put water in slow cooker.
- Mix cayenne pepper, black pepper, salt, garlic, celery, bell pepper, onion, okra, chicken, sausage and roux in.

- Cover. Cook for 6-7 hours on low.
- Use a spoon to skim off fat.

Nutrition Information

- Calories: 447 calories;
- Sodium: 1083
- Total Carbohydrate: 13
- Cholesterol: 65
- Protein: 24.2
- Total Fat: 33

64. Slow Cooker Veggie Beef Soup With Okra

Serving: 4 | Prep: 20mins | Ready in:

Ingredients

- 1 pound ground beef
- 1/4 cup onion, chopped
- 1 (14.5 ounce) can diced tomatoes, drained
- 1 (14.5 ounce) can Italian diced tomatoes, drained
- 1 (16 ounce) package frozen mixed vegetables
- 1 cup sliced fresh or frozen okra
- 2 potatoes, peeled and chopped
- 1 tablespoon ketchup
- salt and pepper to taste

Direction

- Cook onion and ground beef in skillet on medium heat till onion is tender and beef is evenly brown. Drain grease.
- Mix pepper, salt, ketchup, potatoes, okra, veggies, Italian diced tomatoes, diced tomatoes, onion and beef in a slow cooker. Cover with enough water.
- Cover slow cooker. Cook on low for 4 hours.

Nutrition Information

- Calories: 413 calories;

- Total Fat: 14
- Sodium: 488
- Total Carbohydrate: 44.2
- Cholesterol: 69
- Protein: 27.3

65. South Indian Style Okra Fritters

Serving: 5 | Prep: 15mins | Ready in:

Ingredients

- 1/2 pound okra, finely chopped
- 1 green chile pepper, finely chopped
- 2 tablespoons finely chopped fresh cilantro leaves
- 1 tablespoon shortening
- 1 teaspoon salt, or to taste
- 1 teaspoon grated fresh ginger
- 3 tablespoons rice flour, or as needed
- 1 tablespoon chickpea (garbanzo bean) flour, or as needed
- 2 cups vegetable oil for frying, or as needed

Direction

- In a bowl, mix ginger, salt, shortening, cilantro, green chile pepper and okra. Knead chickpea flour and rice flour into okra mixture to make a stiff dough.
- In big saucepan/deep-fryer, heat oil to 175°C/350°F.
- Wet a hand; use to hold dough ball. From dough ball, break small marble-sized bits; drop into hot oil without overcrowding pan. Fry for 7-10 minutes till crisp and golden brown. Transfer fritters to paper towel-lined plate to drain. Keep cooking till you use all the dough. Refill and reheat oil if needed.

Nutrition Information

- Calories: 145 calories;
- Sodium: 470

- Total Carbohydrate: 9.6
- Cholesterol: 0
- Protein: 1.7
- Total Fat: 11.6

- Protein: 5.3
- Total Fat: 5.8

66. Southern Style Fried Okra

Serving: 8 | Prep: 20mins | Ready in:

Ingredients

- 20 pods okra, sliced in 1/4 inch pieces
- 6 Yukon Gold potatoes, cut into 1-inch pieces
- 2 large sweet onion, cut into 1 inch pieces
- 1 (8.5 ounce) package corn bread/muffin mix (such as Jiffy®)
- 1 cup vegetable oil for frying

Direction

- In a colander, put veggies. Use cold water to rinse. Put into big mixing bowl. In the next step, use your best judgement. Coat all veggies in the bowl with enough corn meal. Lightly toss till veggies are coated in corn meal. If needed, add more corn meal.
- Put oil to cover bottom of a big frying pan. Put pan on medium – medium high heat then heat oil till hot yet not smoking. With some water, wet your fingers then flick water into oil to test if the oil is ready. It's ready when oil immediately sizzles.
- In 1 layer, put veggies in frying pan. Flip over when veggies are golden brown on the bottom. Cook till other side is browned. Put into paper towel-lined bowl to drain the oil. Repeat till all veggies are cooked.

Nutrition Information

- Calories: 236 calories;
- Sodium: 489
- Total Carbohydrate: 41.9
- Cholesterol: 1

67. Spicy Pickled Okra

Serving: 12 | Prep: 30mins | Ready in:

Ingredients

- 3/4 pound fresh okra
- 4 1/2 cups cider vinegar
- 2 cups water
- 3 cloves chopped garlic
- 1/4 cup crushed red pepper flakes
- 1/4 cup smoked paprika
- 4 1/2 teaspoons salt
- 1 tablespoon Szechuan peppercorns (optional)

Direction

- Wash okra, lightly rubbing to remove fuzz and grit. Sterilize 2 1-qt. canning jars and lids for minimum of 10 minutes in boiling water. Cool before filling them with okra.
- Boil peppercorns, salt, smoked paprika, red pepper flakes, garlic, water and cider vinegar in big pot on medium high heat; lower temperature. Simmer for 15 minutes then take off heat.
- Loosely pack cleaned, fresh okra in jars; put hot brine on okra, filling jars to the top and seal jars. Make sure the jar rims are clean from residue. Store jars in the fridge. Let contents pickle for minimum of 1 week before serving but 2 weeks is best.

Nutrition Information

- Calories: 46 calories;
- Total Carbohydrate: 6.3
- Cholesterol: 0
- Protein: 1.4
- Total Fat: 0.9
- Sodium: 882

68. Stuffed Okra

Serving: 4 | Prep: 15mins | Ready in:

Ingredients

- 2 tablespoons mango powder (amchur)
- 1 teaspoon ground ginger
- 1 teaspoon ground cumin
- 1 teaspoon ground turmeric
- 1/2 teaspoon chili powder (optional)
- 1/2 teaspoon salt
- 1/2 teaspoon vegetable oil
- 1 pound large okra
- 1/4 cup corn flour
- vegetable oil for frying

Direction

- In a bowl, mix 1/2 tsp. oil, salt, chili powder, turmeric, cumin, ginger and mango powder; put aside for 2 hours to merge flavors.
- In deep fryer/big saucepan, heat vegetable oil to 175°C/350°F.
- Trim okra; create a slit lengthwise down a side of each okra to make a pocket. Use spice mixture to fill each pocket.
- In resealable plastic bag, put corn flour; add filled okra. Shake till coated.
- In hot oil, fry okra for 5-8 minutes till golden brown. Use a slotted spoon to put fried okra on paper towel-lined plate.

Nutrition Information

- Calories: 200 calories;
- Sodium: 307
- Total Carbohydrate: 22.3
- Cholesterol: 0
- Protein: 3.2
- Total Fat: 12.2

69. Summer's Best Grilled Okra

Serving: 6 | Prep: 10mins | Ready in:

Ingredients

- cooking spray
- 1 pound fresh okra
- 1/4 cup canola oil
- 1 teaspoon garlic powder
- 1/2 teaspoon salt
- 1/4 teaspoon ground black pepper

Direction

- Preheat the grill to medium heat. Oil the grate lightly. Prepare a grill basket with cooking spray.
- Trim the end of the stem of the okra near the top without piercing the pods and put it in a big bowl.
- Drizzle canola oil on it. Season it with pepper, salt and garlic powder and toss the okra to coat. In the prepared grill basket, spread the okra.
- For 4 to 6 minutes, cook on the preheated grill. Turn in frequently in between until tender and turns brown in spots.

Nutrition Information

- Calories: 108 calories;
- Total Fat: 9.4
- Sodium: 201
- Total Carbohydrate: 5.7
- Cholesterol: 0
- Protein: 1.6

70. Sylvia's Butterbeans And Okra

Serving: 8 | Prep: 5mins | Ready in:

Ingredients

- 7 cups water, or as needed
- 1 pound dried baby lima beans (butter beans)
- 1 pound pickled pork shoulder, cubed
- 1 onion, chopped
- 1 tablespoon minced garlic
- 1/4 cup butter
- salt and pepper to taste
- 1 (10 ounce) package frozen cut okra

Direction

- In a soup pot, mix together garlic, onion, pork, butter beans and water and boil over medium heat. Cook for 40 minutes. Add pepper, salt and butter; keep boiling for 20 minutes. Add okra; cook for 10 minutes till okra and beans are tender.

Nutrition Information

- Calories: 331 calories;
- Total Fat: 11.7
- Sodium: 67
- Total Carbohydrate: 39.5
- Cholesterol: 38
- Protein: 18.4

71. Texas Okra Gumbo

Serving: 12 | Prep: 30mins | Ready in:

Ingredients

- 6 slices bacon, cut into 1 inch pieces
- 1 onion, diced
- 4 skinless, boneless chicken breast halves - cut into 1 inch cubes
- 2 (16 ounce) packages frozen cut okra
- 10 fresh cayenne peppers, chopped (optional)
- 1 (14.5 ounce) can diced tomatoes with juice
- 2 (10 ounce) cans diced tomatoes with green chile peppers
- 1 cup long grain white rice
- 3 cups water

Direction

- In a Dutch oven or big pot, put the bacon over medium-high heat. Cook it until it turns evenly brown. Add the okra, chicken cubes and the onion. Cook for about 15 minutes until chicken is tender. Stirring in between.
- Mix in the diced tomatoes with green chilies, tomatoes and the cayenne peppers. Put the water and the rice. Turn heat to medium-low heat. For 20 minutes, let it simmer or until the rice is tender.

Nutrition Information

- Calories: 186 calories;
- Protein: 14.3
- Total Fat: 3.7
- Sodium: 376
- Total Carbohydrate: 24.5
- Cholesterol: 29

72. Un Slimy Okra

Serving: 2 | Prep: 5mins | Ready in:

Ingredients

- 1/2 pound fresh okra, cut into 1/2 inch slices
- 8 cherry tomatoes, halved
- olive oil
- kosher salt and ground black pepper to taste
- garlic powder to taste
- 1/2 cup panko bread crumbs

Direction

- Preheat the oven to 220 °C or 425 °F.
- In a bowl, put the tomatoes and the okra. Put the olive oil and sprinkle it with the garlic powder, pepper and the kosher salt. Coat it with the oil by stirring it until the vegetables are coated. Put the panko bread crumbs. Stir. On a lightly greased baking sheet, spread the vegetables in. For 13 to 15 minutes, bake it

until the okra is turns slightly brown and the tomatoes are soft.

Nutrition Information

- Calories: 179 calories;
- Total Fat: 8
- Sodium: 347
- Total Carbohydrate: 30.2
- Cholesterol: 0
- Protein: 5.8

73. Vegan Caribbean Stew

Serving: 6 | Prep: 30mins | Ready in:

Ingredients

- 1 cup uncooked brown rice
- water
- 1/2 pound collard greens, chopped
- 2 cloves garlic, peeled
- 1 (10 ounce) package frozen okra
- 1 (28 ounce) can whole peeled tomatoes, chopped, with liquid
- 1 chayote squash, diced
- 2 cloves garlic, crushed
- 1/4 teaspoon ground ginger, or more to taste
- 1/4 teaspoon dried dill weed, or more to taste
- 1/4 teaspoon ground cumin, or to taste
- 1 tablespoon chopped fresh cilantro, or to taste
- 1 (16 ounce) can kidney beans, rinsed and drained
- 1 (6 ounce) can tomato paste
- all-purpose flour, or as needed

Direction

- In a saucepan, cook brown rice and let it boil in a high fire. Lower down heat to medium-low, place cover and let it simmer for 45 to 50 minutes until the rice becomes tender and the water is absorbed.

- In a pot, put 2 peeled whole garlic clove and collard greens then fill it with sufficient water to cover. Let it boil for about 15 minutes until collards become tender. Drain.
- In another big pot, mix chayote squash, two crushed garlic cloves, tomatoes and okra. Let it boil and cook for about 5 minutes until okra is melted. Lower down to simmer, spice with cilantro, ground ginger, ground cumin and dill weed to add taste. Mix in collard greens and let it simmer for at least 40 minutes to 60 minutes to achieve best flavors until all are blended.
- In a bowl, puree kidney beans with tomato paste then put into the stew. Mix cooked rice then stir together. If desired, put a spoonful of flour to make it thick. Check taste and balance seasonings.

Nutrition Information

- Calories: 235 calories;
- Sodium: 218
- Total Carbohydrate: 48.8
- Cholesterol: 0
- Protein: 10.5
- Total Fat: 1.5

74. Vendakka Paalu

Serving: 2 | Prep: 15mins | Ready in:

Ingredients

- 2 tablespoons olive oil
- 1/2 bell pepper, seeded and sliced into strips
- 2 jalapeno peppers, seeded and sliced into strips
- 1 tablespoon minced fresh ginger root
- 1 tablespoon minced garlic
- 2 bay leaves
- 1 teaspoon ground coriander
- 1/2 teaspoon ground red pepper
- 1/4 teaspoon ground turmeric

- 1/4 teaspoon cumin seeds
- 1/8 teaspoon ground cardamom
- 1/8 teaspoon ground black pepper
- 1/8 teaspoon ground cinnamon
- 1 small tomato, sliced
- 1/4 cup golden raisins
- 1 cup sliced okra
- 1 cup coconut milk
- 1 tablespoon water
- salt to taste

Direction

- In a big skillet, heat the oil. Stir the bell pepper. Cook for about 3 minutes until it slightly softens. Add the bay leaves, garlic, ginger and jalapeno peppers into the bell pepper. For about 2 to 3 minutes more, cook until fragrant. Season it with cinnamon, black pepper, cardamom, cumin seeds, turmeric, red pepper and coriander. For another 2 minutes, cook and stir it. Put the tomato slices and raisins into the mixture and continue cooking for 3 more minutes. Put the okra. Mix thoroughly into the mixture to coat with the spices.
- In a small bowl, stir the water and the coconut milk together. Put it into the mixture then, cover the skillet. Cook for 8 to 10 minutes until the okra is tender. To keep it moist, add water if needed. Season it with salt. Serve it warm.

Nutrition Information

- Calories: 456 calories;
- Cholesterol: 0
- Protein: 5.5
- Total Fat: 38.4
- Sodium: 27
- Total Carbohydrate: 30.5

75. Zesty Baked Gluten Free, Corn Free Okra

Serving: 4 | Prep: 10mins | Ready in:

Ingredients

- 1 serving cooking spray
- 1 (10 ounce) package frozen okra, thawed and sliced
- 1 tablespoon grapeseed oil, or more as needed
- 1/2 cup gluten-free flour
- 1 teaspoon smoked paprika
- 1/2 teaspoon salt
- 1 pinch dried crushed oregano
- 1 pinch dried crushed thyme
- 1 pinch chipotle pepper powder
- freshly ground black pepper to taste

Direction

- Preheat oven to 230°C or 450°F. Align the aluminum foil with the baking sheet. Spray it with cooking spray.
- In a big bowl, toss the grapeseed oil and the okra. In a small bowl, mix the pepper, chipotle powder, thyme, oregano, salt, paprika and gluten-free flour. Put flour mixture over the okra. Mix well to combine. On the prepared baking sheet, arrange it in one spread layer.
- For 20 minutes, bake it in the preheated oven. For 10 to 25 more minutes, stir and bake until crisp. Once done, remove it from the oven. Leave it for a few minutes to allow the crispy part to be separated from the foil.

Nutrition Information

- Calories: 113 calories;
- Total Fat: 4.2
- Sodium: 297
- Total Carbohydrate: 18.2
- Cholesterol: 0
- Protein: 3.3

Index

Conclusion

Thank you again for downloading this book!

I hope you enjoyed reading about my book!

If you enjoyed this book, please take the time to share your thoughts and post a review on Amazon. It'd be greatly appreciated!

Write me an honest review about the book – I truly value your opinion and thoughts and I will incorporate them into my next book, which is already underway.

Thank you!

If you have any questions, **feel free to contact at:** _author@soybeanrecipes.com_

Sharon Brown

soybeanrecipes.com

Made in United States
North Haven, CT
21 October 2021

10478289R00026